ISLANDS APART

Becoming Dominican American

Jasminne Mendez

PIÑATA BOOKS
ARTE PÚBLICO PRESS
HOUSTON, TEXAS

Islands Apart: Becoming Dominican American is published in part with support from the Texas Commission on the Arts. We are grateful for its support.

Piñata Books are full of surprises!

Piñata Books
An imprint of
Arte Público Press
University of Houston
4902 Gulf Fwy, Bldg. 19, Rm 100
Houston, Texas 77204-2004

Cover design by Mora Des¡gn
Artwork © 2022 by Gaby D'Alessandro

Library of Congress Control Number: 2022934356

Printed in the United States of America
May 2022–August 2022
Versa Press, Inc., East Peoria, IL
5 4 3 2 1

TABLE OF CONTENTS

For Luz María

AT DAYBREAK

Alabama. 1984. Mami is very pregnant.

Open your eyes and breathe life into your belly.

Papi is working the night shift as a guard on base
and his gaze is on the moonlight hovering over
Mami's room in the barracks across the street.
She came with him "por si acaso."

Gaze at the moonlight. Let the covers hover over
your bare shoulders, curl up to the warmness of you,
hum a birdsong quiet as dawn, and linger
there a little bit longer "just in case."

Mami groans. A contraction.
She calls Papi but his name staccatos
on the way out of her mouth. "Ben-ja-mín!" She hums.
Another contraction. It lingers. She hums. It lingers.
The contractions make her sing. Papi is nowhere to be
found.
The lingering hum.

Sing into the spine of your body
and wait until the alarm chimes.
Your bones bend, snap and staccato—
the melody of the broken queuing up as you reach
out and turn it off.
Will your limbs to hang idly. Like a
a weeping willow tree.

Mami's voice crescendos. My two-year-old brother,
Ben, wakes up weeping—his own like a willow tree.
Mami moans. She rubs the pain to a stillness. My brother
Ben weeps some more. Papi sits idly by, too far away to
    hear.
Mami becomes weary.

Become weary. Understand what it means to swell like
water,
rise out of bed anyway, groan with heavy fingers and wake
your eyes free from the dirt of night. Smell the
morning heat
and speak into the silence of you. Let your feet float
like mist off the side of the bed. Hollowed and wasted,
decide to
give your brutal body a chance. It's time.

Mami's melodies break the silence
down the hall, echoing a call
that prompts the staff supervisor to come to her aide.
In English that cuts like grass, like an out of tune guitar,
Mami explains to the white woman:

"Baby! *Es* coming! Baby! *¡Estoy teniendo un bebé!*"

              "Baby," he says. "Are you all right?" Lie.
       Nod. Contemplate life, if only briefly. Breathe.
      It's coming, the pain that chokes you. Breathe.
             This can't last forever. Breathe.
             Cradle yourself and breathe.

I'm soon to arrive. Mami is in labor.
"Breathe," the woman tells her.
Mami knows this can't last forever. So she
breathes. The woman leaves to get Papi.
Mami swallows the pain and waddles
to the other side of the room, hands steady on the red
   brick wall,
and her water breaks like a *river falling out of heaven,*
as natural as heavy dew.

                    At daybreak,
rush to the bathroom and let a warm river fall. Breathe.
  A sigh of relief. A sign of life. Hold your heavy hands
                      steady.
  Open a window and let the scent of jasmines smother
                  you back to life.

The woman and Papi return.
Mami breathes a sigh of relief.
Their white and black and white and brown and black
   hands

smother themselves around Mami's waist
to help her into the car. She breathes.
Two hours later, a sign of life emerges, they will name
    me Jasminne and I . . .

        Make a grand entrance into the world.

THE CHICKEN POX

Itchy. Red. Hot. I was hot but wanted and needed . . .
to go . . . to school. It was the Christmas gift exchange.
We had bought a Barbie. With brown hair and brown
eyes. A dress and heels. Like all the pretty girls.

The cold wind blew. I itched. So itchy. Was hot.
101.3 degrees. A fever. Mami said no. I cried. *¿Por qué?*
I wanted and needed to go. Stomping feet. Tears, red
hot. Clenched fist. Itchy knuckles, red hot. Mami caved.
"*Está bien*," she said.

Covered in pink calamine. I was itchy, hot and pink
and wrapped in a silk scarf. I was wrapped head to toe.
Black wool gloves. Black tight leggings scratching my
thighs, rubbing across knees and scraping my toes.
Itchy and hot. Too hot. But I wanted to go . . . to go . . .
to school. Wanted and needed. My gift was waiting.

The cold wind blew across my face like shattered
pieces of glass. It pierced my itchy, hot skin. Gift in
hand, I arrived at the Christmas party on time. I broke
out in a cold sweat.

"Come here," my teacher said, "Take off the scarf."
I wouldn't. No.
Now in my face, she said, "Come closer."
No, no, no.

I was sent to the office. No bell had rung. No pledge to the flag. No . . . gift . . . no exchange. Red skin burning. Tears falling like snowflakes.

The cold wind blew. Mom came back. She said, "*Ya te lo dije.* I told you so. Let's go."

Time to go . . . to go home.

ကာ ကာ

The first time I remember being sick was also the first Christmas I remember. I've dubbed it the chicken pox Christmas because it was then that my body felt things my poor five-year-old self couldn't handle. I trembled and cried. I remember trying to smile when Papi came home with our gifts. I don't recall what they were, but I know that at some point amid the itching and scratching and tears, and Mami's frustration and Papi's exhaustion, there was joy.

"*Ven aquí*," Mami said as she pulled my itchy and red-hot blistering arm towards her and dragged me into the tub, "*y no te rasques.*" She told me if I kept scratching, I would get scars. But the itching was unbearable, so I scratched without regret.

I winced at her touch as she placed me in the tub and I felt the tears well up in my eyes but knew that crying would only upset her more. I swallowed my pain and discomfort and sank into the tub. The water was lukewarm and felt holy against my blistered skin. I took a deep breath and sat down. Mami began to lather me up with oatmeal soap. She looked tired, her normally vibrant brown skin and bright eyes looked sunken and hollow. Her hands felt soft and fleshy like my abuela's from working with water washing dishes, clothes and people by hand for too long. As she rubbed the wash-cloth over me, her forehead glistened. She wiped her brow with the sleeve of her pink and blue floral robe and her normally straight and blown-out roots began to frizz from the humidity and warmth that enveloped us both. I knew we both were tired enough to cry. But somehow, whether for each other or for ourselves, we held it together.

Mami scrubbed and patted and rinsed. Scrubbed and patted and rinsed. All I wanted in that moment was for Mami to make the itching go away. I know that's all she was trying to do, but it still felt like a million fire ants were crawling all over my body. My body clenched and I squeezed my face shut. Mami told me to relax, but I couldn't. I wanted to scratch so badly, but her grip on me was tight, and I didn't want to make her mad.

"*Te vas a sentir mejor. Cálmate, no es nada.*" She was trying to reduce my fever and soothe me the best way she knew. She kept telling me to relax. That's when I started to cry.

"*¿Por qué lloras? No es nada. Ya. No llores, Yamina.*" She wiped my tears with her soggy, wrinkled hands. I sniffled and choked on the water running down my face into my mouth.

"*Pero me pica.* It itches." I squirmed in the tub, sobbed and kicked my feet, splashing milky water every-where. I was five and believed tantrums were called for. Mami didn't feel the same way. She yanked my arm and told me to stop throwing a fit. She said she was almost done and that all of this was "*por tu bien,*" for my own good. I pouted, tears and water streaming down my face. I let her finish.

When she picked me up and wrapped me in the towel, my skin ached. I could feel each hair follicle throbbing to the rhythm of my breath. My veins pulsated and I could hear the thump-thump of my heart in my ears. I thought my body would burst and my insides would ooze out onto the bathroom floor, leaving a huge mess for Mami to mop up.

The thought of Mami cleaning me up off the tile made me start to cry again. I quickly wiped my face with the towel before she noticed. She grabbed a clean washcloth, sat on the toilet and began to slather me with calamine lotion for the third time that day. It felt cool. It was soothing. For a moment I didn't need to scratch. She half-smiled at me, wiped her forehead with her sleeve, rolled her neck and exhaled, trying to release the stress of the day. She told me to get dressed. Once dressed, I looked in the full-length mirror on my closet door and saw what looked like a giant pink lollipop. I was in a fuchsia, onesie-footed pajama set and all I could see was my bright pink face and my cracked pink hands. It would've made me laugh if my skin wasn't throbbing and my throat didn't hurt so much.

Mami then called my older brother, Ben, who was next in line for his own round of oatmeal soap, calamine lotion and fifteen minutes of distress. My little sister Jenny had finally fallen asleep after a few grueling hours of tears, screaming and inconsolable whining, so Mami wanted to take advantage of the short break to give us both a bath while she still could.

I can't imagine what it must've been like for Mami to take care of three children with chicken pox during the Christmas holidays. We couldn't go anywhere or do anything. All of us were housebound. The doctors had given us what medicine they could and told us to go home and let it play out.

Between oatmeal baths, layers of anti-itch creams and lotions, intervals of children's Tylenol and the occasional chicken soup and *sancocho* that we could hold down, Mami barely slept. After three days of it all, she was finally at her wit's end. She had no time or patience for tears or tantrums and just wanted all three of us to get better as quickly as possible. She nurtured us in her practical "eat well, sleep well, drink enough fluids" kind of way and spoiled us by letting us watch as much English TV as we wanted. Although she normally loved to cook and host holiday parties and dinners for a full house of friends and family, that year she had resigned herself to a quiet, uneventful Christmas at home. Even so, she still believed there could be some way to salvage the holiday season and spirit. She knew she could make the magic of Christmas happen for us if she could reduce our fevers and get us to keep something down. Her only Christmas wish that year was to have enough energy and strength to mother us back to perfect health.

When Mami finished our baths, my brother and I went to the living room and curled up on the couch. Exhausted from the endless marathon of itching, sweating and breaking a fever, we could do nothing more than stare at the TV and try to make sense of the cartoon images that filled the screen.

"*¿Quieren algo de comer?*" Mami asked hopefully with genuine concern and love. She knew we could only regain our strength if we were properly nourished, but food was the last thing on our minds. We shook our heads no and held our empty bellies. She wrapped us up in warm fleece blankets and brought us juice. We all sat on the couch watching violent cartoon reruns of Bugs Bunny and Speedy Gonzales while Mami nodded off between commercials and checked our temperatures and offered us food.

When Papi got home that night, he asked how we were. We moaned and groaned and scratched. Mami scolded us and moved our hands off our bodies to stop scratching. Papi asked if there was anything he could do for us to make us feel less sad. There was only one thing all three of us wanted. Only one thing we had already tried once to conspire and get, but failed: candy.

It was Christmas Eve. That meant that the local fire department would drive through the streets of the little Louisiana town we were living in at the time and spread the holiday spirit by throwing candy to all the children who came outside to see Santa Claus on the fire truck. Despite our protestations, pleading and prayers, Mami and Papi had already told us several times that week that going outside to the cold was out of the question.

When Papi asked what it was we wanted, Mami said, "*Quieren dulces. No han comido nada todo el día, pero quieren dulces.*" She had revealed our deepest desires. She then got up from the couch, folded her blanket and set it on the arm of a chair, sighed and yawned and walked to the kitchen.

We looked up at Papi from beneath our blankets, calamine lotion cracking on our swollen skin. I think our pain was too much to bear. He called after Mami and said we looked abandoned and destitute.

"*Pero, Sonia, mira estos muchachos. Unos dulces no le van a hacer daño.*"

ISLANDS APART 11

My heart fluttered with anticipation. After seeing our sunken eyes and tired expressions, Papi was finally on our side. He knew a little candy wouldn't harm us any worse than what we already felt. So when the fire truck came up our street, Papi threw on his coat and rushed outside to get the candy for us. Ben and I kneeled on the sofa and spread the curtains wide to see out the window. Jenny stood up between us but still couldn't really see.

The sirens outside blared, the horn honked and all the neighborhood kids stood in their driveways or on the street waving their arms at the Christmas parade, trying to catch whatever flew overhead. For the first time that week, I smiled.

As the truck pulled closer to our house, Papi also began to wave his hands. I saw his mouth move but I couldn't hear what he was saying. I realized that Santa and the firemen weren't giving him any candy. He waved his hands some more and pointed back to the house. I imagined he told them all about his sick children and their lonely Christmas. I imagined he used what little broken English he had to explain that the candy wasn't for him but for his poor, sick children in the house. The men looked at the window Papi was pointing at, where we poked our heads through the curtains and looked like three bobble-headed dashboard dolls. Before I knew it, they thrust a handful of candy at Papi and drove off. We bounced up and down on the couch. Mami laughed and then told us to calm down as she closed the curtain. She covered us back up with our blankets and once again moved our scratching fingers away from our arms and legs. We sat giggling, all tucked in on the couch, our legs squirming and our bodies still bouncing up and down as we waited for Papi to return. He came in a few moments later with his hands and pockets full. He smiled like he was Santa incarnate.

"Damn, it's cold. *¡Qué frío del diablo!*"

He emptied the contents of his hands and pockets onto the coffee table. We wanted to rush towards it, but knew Mami wouldn't let us eat any without having dinner first. Our legs shook and our sad smiles morphed into big grins in anticipation of eating even just one piece of candy. It made us forget all about the blisters and sores, the uneasiness and the pain.

Mami saw our enthusiasm but said we had to eat and set the table. She served us steaming bowls of *sancocho* broth. As we slurped the soup, burning our tongues with every bite, I saw Mami place her hand on top of Papi's. They both shook their heads at us and sighed. With Papi's simple excursion, Mami's Christmas wish and our Christmas wishes had come true. Even though this wasn't the type of Dominican island Christmas with loud *merengue,* noisy neighbors, oven-roasted fresh ham and *pernil*, that Mami and Papi were used to, we all felt nourished. We all felt a moment of grace. We all felt like this could be home.

ENGLISH AS A SECOND LANGUAGE

The South. We lived in the Deep South until I was twelve. I was born on the east side of the Mississippi River in Alabama. I spent grade school at several different Army-base towns: three years in New Llano, Louisiana, and four years on the border of Clarksville, Tennessee and Ft. Campbell, Kentucky. Aside from our brief stint in Germany, we always lived in the Deep South. Somehow, despite our varied shades of dark and darker, we were always Dominican. No one said anything about us being black. We ate *plátanos* and *arroz con leche*. Mami put *rolos* in my hair. I learned to dance *bachata* while standing on my father's toes. We celebrated Nochebuena with *pernil* and *Mamá Juana*, the Dominican national liquor, and we always spoke Spanish at home.

It was 1988, we were living in New Llano, a place where bilingual education and ESL—English as a Second Language—classes were a thing of the future. In New Llano, you were either black or white, and everyone spoke English. We fit into the category of black. I went to school speaking only Spanish. The English of my teachers and classmates sounded at times soft and soothing like a *bolero* or ballad, other times like a broken cuckoo clock, loud and aggressive. I understood their inflections and intonations, even if I couldn't grasp the meaning of their words.

The idea of anyone speaking anything other than Spanish was so foreign to us that during the first parent-teacher conference, my kindergarten teacher asked Papi if I was deaf. She was a young white woman, probably born and raised in Louisiana herself, with a kind smile and good intentions. When she asked Papi if I was deaf, he cocked his head to the side, wrinkled his brow and in his own cracked and rough English said, "No, why do you ask?"

"Because I speak to her and she just stares at me. I mean, she doesn't cause any trouble, but she never answers my questions. She just stares at me." The rookie Kindergarten teacher could not make sense of why a little Black girl was not able to speak or understand English.

Papi laughed. "No, no, she's not deaf. She just doesn't understand you. She doesn't speak English."

"Oh, well, what DOES she speak?"

"*Espanish.*"

"Oh."

Papi laughed once again and told her not to worry. He was confident I would pick up the language easily, just as he had, and that he and my brother, who was already in second grade and fluent, would practice with me at home. He was right, I did learn English right away. By December of that school year, I was as fluent in English as any other kid in my class. The words and the sounds no longer ached in my ears or stumbled on my tongue.

After Louisiana, we were stationed in Nuremburg, Germany, for two years. However, I didn't learn German because we lived on the military base, where we went to an English-language school with other American military brats. Whenever we were adventurous enough to travel off base, German words sounded like fireworks against my ears. It was rough and scary and reminded me of the old World War II movies I loathed. I wanted nothing to do with German.

After our brief stay overseas, we were transferred to Ft. Campbell, Kentucky, close to where my parents bought a house off base in Clarksville, Tennessee. By then I was headed to middle school. In the sixth grade I decided I wanted to learn how to play the alto saxophone. I had grown up watching *The Simpsons*, and Bill Clinton was president at the time. I wanted to be just like Lisa Simpson and Bill—intelligent, great people.

But learning to play that instrument was not as easy as I had expected. The stray black shapes placed on the page were a foreign language to me, much like English had been and how German always was. The notes were translated into letters I understood, E, G, B, D, F and into phrases I could repeat on command: "Every good boy does fine." Yet my ears could not distinguish the different notes. *What did the keys on my sax have to do with the circles and lines that dripped up and down like black wax on the page?* I could make sounds on the sax that made sense, but I wasn't really making music.

I used my diaphragm to blow out forced staccatos and belabored half notes that dragged on too long or were cut too short. I filled the spaces of my brass sax with flat whole notes that would decrescendo simply because I lacked the confidence to play with vibrato and strength. For the first three months, I fine-tuned the art of faking it. I listened to those around me for when to stop and when to pick it back up. I labeled the notes on the page with their corresponding letters, and followed along, like watching a foreign film with the English sub-titles. I read *above* the notes but failed to look *at* them. In the end, the notes rested on the page like migrating birds on a wire, interesting to look at but meaningless to me.

It took me three months to learn how to read sheet music and play the saxophone. Just like it had taken me three months in kindergarten to learn English. I worked hard at both because I wanted to fit in. I wanted to be a part of the club, the "I'm an American" club. The band club. The "I promise I'm just like you even though I'm black and speak Spanish" club. The "I'm normal like everyone else" club. I needed to speak English, and to learn to read music, because I needed to feel included. I needed to feel like everyone else. Language was the only way.

I decided at the age of eleven or twelve to try to understand why I was not allowed to speak English to my parents. I knew Spanish was my first language. I knew Mami didn't speak English. But English, to me, felt so much easier. I spoke English at school and with my siblings. I liked English, it was on TV, it was spoken out in the world, and it was in the books I read and loved. I thought in English, I dreamt in English and I sang in English. I wanted to speak English with Mami and Papi because I knew more words in English. I even felt in English! I did not know the Spanish words for ostracized, bullied and melancholic. My eleven-year-old vocabulary in English far exceeded my conversational Spanish and I couldn't understand why this language was forbidden with Mami and Papi. My brain had to think and work in two languages just to be heard and understood. I had to translate for Mami at the store, "¿Cuánto cuesta?"; at the hairdresser, "Dile que no me gusta"; and at the mall, "Dile que quiero un tamaño más grande." This chore alone was exhausting. If they only would have learned English and we all spoke it at home, then everything would have been easier.

So I asked Papi in Spanish one day, "Why do we have to keep speaking Spanish at home? In America, everyone speaks English." He was sitting in his recliner, a book propped on his lap as usual and a cold beer in his hand. He was still partially dressed in his uniform, wearing his brown and green camouflage pants and his chocolate covered undershirt, stained with sweat. He wrinkled his forehead and narrowed his eyes but he smiled slyly. Then he looked at me from above his reading glasses.

Like a parent repeating step-by-step instructions to a small child for the third time, he said, "When you go into an interview for a job, knowing Spanish will be your advantage, because they will need you." He closed his three-hundred page book and sat up, shifting his weight onto his elbow and straightening his palm so all of his words could flow through his hands. "Having a degree will not be enough." His hand hacked at me sternly. "Being bilingual, *te va a ayudar*."

His eyes traced my body up and down, left and right. He pointed at me with his calloused, ashy index finger and proclaimed, "In order to compete with others in this world, *tú tienes que ser más, hacer más y saber más que ellos*. It's the only way," he said, "*que vas a poder progresar en este mundo*. So if I want to get anywhere in this world, I have to know more and be more than other people? I assumed he said it because I was Latina, because after all he didn't say anything about being black. But whatever the reason, it didn't seem fair.

SHE WAS LINDA

My best friend Linda was an imaginary American girl with bouncy brown hair, brown eyes, long lashes, and small round hands with fingernails that were always painted pink. She also had peppermint breath and pure white porcelain skin that always smelled like cornbread. It didn't matter that no one else could see her. I saw her vividly. She wore designer OshKosh B'gosh floral dresses with silk periwinkle purple and baby blue bows on the sleeves or tied around the waist. She always kept her black leather Mary Jane shoes clean, despite running around the yard with me for hours and she was always there when I needed someone to play with or talk to. She was my best friend from the age of four to eight, until Papi got stationed in Germany and I had to leave her behind.

I chose to make Linda everything I was not: wealthy, beautiful, straight-haired, white and American. Linda was also allowed to do all the things I was not. Mami never let me paint my nails or leave my hair down or wear my "good clothes" to play outside. I always chewed off my nails out of boredom. Mami always braided my thick curly hair into five braids or more. And the scratchy polyester dresses I owned could only be worn to Mass on Sundays or on special occasions, like Christmas or New Year's. I did have a few everyday dresses, but they were nothing like Linda's. My thin discount dresses hung limply on my frail, petite body and definitely didn't twirl and catch the wind the way Linda's always did when she spun around.

Despite our differences, we were inseparable. Wherever I went, there she was, like a shadow waiting for me to talk to her or play with her or whisper another secret into her unpierced ears. That was the one small advantage I had over her. Mami had my ears pierced in the hospital the day after I was born. It is a customary Dominican tradition to pierce girls' ears young, so they don't cry and fuss as much. It's also one of the only small details that lets strangers know your baby is female. Linda, on the other hand, was American. Most American white girls aren't allowed to get their ears pierced until they're older. I learned this by chance after I started school and noticed that most of my classmates walked around earring-less, like boys. I found it odd and even scandalous that in elementary school they couldn't wear earrings but had the privilege of having "boyfriends," wearing nail polish, short skirts, heels and sometimes even lipstick! Mami had always warned me that I was not allowed any of those things until I became a *señorita,* and although at the time I didn't know what that meant, Mami assured me that that probably wouldn't happen until after I turned fifteen. Besides, she told me once, "Don't bother asking me for permission, because Papi won't allow it, anyway." So while I envied Linda's and all the other American girl's early entrance into the world of womanhood, I knew I was special because I was one of the few whose ears were pierced.

Linda and I could play and talk and make believe for hours. We'd run back and forth playing chase and tag in the backyard. We played house, doctor and school in Papi's toolshed. And after my brother Ben showed us that there were edible plants on the side of the house, we'd sit in the dirt and pluck mint leaves from the ground until our teeth were stained green and our fingertips smelled like candy canes. We'd eat it by the fistful, giggling uncontrollably as we brushed dirt and ants off the leaves, believing we were breaking some unknown rule or law for eating things out of the ground without Mami or Papi knowing about it.

Linda jumped rope with me when my brother and sister were busy with something else. I could always count on her to join me for teatime with Barbie and Ken, Teddy Bear, My Little Pony and Miss Piglet. Sometimes Linda would even talk to me before I fell asleep, but I could never remember what she said. And when no one else would sit with me on the bus, I could always count on Linda to fill the silence or the space between me and everyone else. Linda wasn't real, but she made my world feel a lot less lonely. She allowed me to believe that I wasn't as different as everyone else made me feel, that I could be accepted by the white American girls with perfect skin and perfect hair and perfect clothes. And I knew that if they accepted me then, maybe I too would be just as beautiful and as perfect and as American as them one day.

Although I stopped imagining and conjuring Linda up at about the age of eight, I would see her face in the

American Girl doll look-alikes I would try to befriend for the rest of my life. I found Linda's hair in the middle school beauty pageant queen Elsie, who let me sit with her at lunch because I complimented her often and knew how to braid her board-straight locks on command. I looked for the love and affection Linda gave me in my high school frenemy Laura Killian. Laura and I were in drama class together and she was the cute and lovable "girl next door" type who was cast in every lead role in every play we ever auditioned for together. I was inevitably always cast as her nurse, her teacher, her maid or her stagehand. The real "Lindas" of the world taunted me. In my college years, they were the sorority girls that lived in my dorm hall but never came to say hello. They were the group of white girls at the club staring down at me and my black friends when we danced and they stood at the bar holding a drink. So many of these American white girls looked like my Linda, but they weren't her, not even close.

These girls were indifferent to my acts of kindness and goodwill towards them. They used me for answers on homework assignments and tests. They used me to carry the weight of group projects and as an alibi when they wanted to go out with their boyfriends and needed an ally to corroborate their lies to Mom and Dad. In college, they used me to drop them off and pick them up from parties where they'd gotten too drunk and were left abandoned by their other friends. I knew I was being taken advantage of, but I also felt empowered. I wasn't the only intelligent and capable girl at school that they knew, so why choose me? I knew there were other girls that would have been willing to help them just to be a part of the popular crowd. I knew I wasn't the only black girl, the only nerdy girl, the only girl seeking validation that would've sacrificed a little dignity just to fit in. But for whatever reason, despite the many options they had to choose from, they all came to me. So I knew that as much as I wanted their approval, they needed my abilities to be the kind of girls that "had it all."

But as I grew older, these Linda impersonators wanted to be seen in public with me less and less. They called on me and talked to me in secluded and desolate places when their other friends weren't around. They didn't make eye contact with me in the hallways, and I was never invited to join them at birthday parties, the movies, or the mall. I eventually learned to stop answering their calls and I started investing time in the people that looked like me and spoke like me. I made more male friends than female friends and felt distrustful and weary of the black and Latina girls that did want to talk to and spend time with me. I was skeptical because I thought they had ulterior motives and would eventually spurn me for someone prettier, someone "better," someone more American. By the time I was in my late teens and early twenties, however, I realized that all us "colored" girls feared the same thing because at some point in our lives we had all been betrayed or used by our "all-American white girlfriends."

Right before we moved to Germany, I realized that I would need to start making "real" friends. I couldn't hide out alone in the toolshed or talk to myself on the bus anymore. Kids were already starting to make fun of me, and teachers had begun to express their "concern" about my solitude. So one afternoon, I walked outside to the barren peach tree that stood in our front yard and said goodbye to Linda. I'm not sure what compelled me to the tree that day, but as I walked up to it, I kicked the dirt and mumbled things I don't recall. Maybe I said a prayer, maybe it was a mini tantrum for knowing this was goodbye, maybe it was nothing more than the words to a childhood song. All I know for sure is that I didn't want to be walking up to that tree, but I knew it was time. Things were changing. Papi had told us we were moving again—this was the third move in my short eight years of life—and I knew that this time I couldn't take Linda with me. It was time to let her go.

I leaned up against the tree and began:

"Linda, I'm sorry, but you have to go now."

Linda's face grew dark. Her fluffy dress seemed to wilt and go limp on her translucent body. She was already disappearing. Silence filled the space between us. I felt a breeze and smelled the mint leaves from her breath. A small dark cloud covered the sun, and thunder crashed somewhere far away. I sighed, stared at the trunk of the tree and let my eyes follow a trail of ants into a patch of dead grass. Linda wouldn't say anything, and I didn't know how to say goodbye. I didn't know how to grieve yet. I kicked at the dirt between us. Her soft brown hair seemed to be dissolving with the wind. I looked at her one last time.

Before I could imagine Linda's response or feel the guilt of letting her go, Mami pushed the screen door open and called for me to come inside because it looked like it was going to rain. I ran into the house and let the screen door shut behind me. When I turned around, Linda was gone. She was the first of only a few all-American white girls to ever show me kindness. She was the only one I would ever consider a best friend.

As I matured, I was able to separate myself from the other imaginary Lindas of the world that kept me a secret and took up space without giving me any consideration in return. I eventually stopped looking for the physical Linda that I imagined in ivory faces, "good" hair and designer clothes. I had to trust myself to find sisterhood with my future Puerto Rican best friend Crystal, with my closeted gay best friend Diego, revel in the laugh of my soul sister Shameka and the companionship of my college roommate Camryn. Linda found her way into all these people who taught me that what I wanted and needed from people, from the world, and from America, was to feel . . . REAL.

VALENTINE'S DAY

A black boy named Jasmine gave me flowers once, a teddy bear and a piece of jewelry I couldn't accept. He was a boy in my third-grade class who had a crush on me, I think because we shared the same name. It was the first time I'd ever met anyone else with my name, but I didn't understand it because Jasmine was a girl's name. All the kids made fun of him. *I* made fun of him. Because of his name. Because he was skinny and nerdy and awkward and shy. I never said anything to his face, but I laughed at him behind his back when the others called him names and pushed him out of the lunch line.

I didn't see myself in him. I too was awkward and confused and not enough of anything. I didn't see that then. I had a few friends, so I thought I was just like everyone else. So I didn't give him a chance. Not because I was mean but because I was afraid. I was afraid of my own black father and what he would do if he found out a boy liked me. I wasn't allowed crushes or boys or love. I was too young. Crushes lead to kissing, kissing leads to sex, sex leads to teen pregnancies. I had to focus on school, from now until . . . who knew? I was told and I understood that boys would come later. Papi's rule was that as long as I lived in his house and didn't pay for my own living expenses, I was not allowed to look at the opposite sex, much less date.

Skinny, friendless Jasmine came to me one morning as we stood in the hall at our pint-sized lockers waiting for the teacher to usher us into class. Despite my alliance with the bullies who taunted him daily, he handed me a Valentine's Day gift.

"Jasminne . . ." he said.

"Hi," I replied looking around, hoping no one would notice we were chatting.

"Here, I got this for you. My mom helped me pick it." He handed me three roses, a brown bear and a small red velvet box.

I took each item, one by one, and admired them silently. No one, especially no boy had ever given me a gift before. I wanted to smile, but I didn't want him to think that I liked him. The roses smelled so fresh, the way Mami's garden did in the summer. The brown bear was so soft and warm, with a furry velvet nose that I wanted to nuzzle. He asked me to open the box. I did slowly. Inside was a dime-sized gold heart on a chain. It caught the light and shimmered. Next to Mami's wedding ring, it was the most beautiful piece of jewelry I'd ever seen. I knew I couldn't keep them. Papi would be so mad if he knew a boy had given me a gift. I hated that.

"Thank you. But I can't take this." I shut the box with a thud louder than I expected. It echoed in the empty hallway. I handed it back to him, hung my head down and noticed that the shoelaces of his oversized New Balance grey and blue tennis shoes were untied. I looked up and was about to tell him to tie his shoes so he wouldn't fall, but he spoke before I could.

"But I got it for you," he said, stroking the velvet box with his thumb. He didn't look me in the eye, probably too embarrassed to have been rejected by his first crush.

"I know, but my dad will be mad. I can't take it home, so I have to return it." It sounded pitiful. And yet, I hadn't returned the roses or the bear, which I held close to my chest and almost hoped he'd let me keep.

Jasmine shuffled his feet and said, "Okay," and started to turn around.

The sight of his hunched shoulders and his frail spine protruding from under his polo shirt pulled at my conscience.

I stepped towards him and said, "Wait, okay, never mind. I'll take it. It's so nice."

He spun back around, his tennis shoes squeaking on the tiled floor, the light returning to his eyes.

I took the box from him quickly and shoved it and the flowers and bear into my locker and thanked him one last time.

Jasmine perked up, and his lips could not contain the oversized teeth that burst through them. He beamed and I looked away. The teacher called us both into the classroom. I sauntered in behind him and took my seat.

That was the only interaction we would ever have. I don't know what became of him or where he went after that school year. I was too afraid to ever take the gifts home because I knew Mami and Papi would ask too many questions and think the worst. I kept the gifts in my locker for the remainder of the year. On the last day of school when we cleaned out our lockers, I crushed the dried flowers in one hand, collected the bear and the necklace in the other and threw them all out.

A Bucket of Dirty Water

"*¡El que manda va dos veces!*" Mami yelled from the bathroom, and I knew that I was in for it. At eleven years old as the eldest daughter, I was being raised to become the perfect housewife and mother. Lately, Mami had insisted that I learn how to "really" clean the bathroom and how to "properly" wash the dishes and clean the kitchen. As usual, Mami had gone in to inspect my work and determine whether or not I would be able to enjoy the rest of my Saturday outside playing, like my older brother and younger sister had been already. Based on her predictable catchphrase, meaning "If you want something done right, you have to do it yourself," I knew that I would probably be on my hands and knees ready to hit the bathroom floor and try again.

"*¿Qué pasó*, Mami?" I sighed, slumped my shoulders and sauntered into the narrow bathroom ready for her "What don't you understand about cleaning it right?"

Mami was holding a banana-yellow and forest-green sponge in her right hand and the blue and white toilet bowl brush in her left. She pointed into the toilet with the brush and began: "*¡¿Tú crees que esto está limpio?!*"—Do you really think this is clean?!

It seemed I had left a few stray chunks of whatever it was Papi pooped into the bowl. Of course, this was not acceptable. Mami said I had *"manos blanditas,"* soft hands. So, she showed me with a forceful grip around the brush handle and with vigor in her forearm how to clean a toilet bowl correctly.

"Mira. Así se hace. ¿Ves?"—You see, that's the way to do it.

She handed me the brush so I could try. And I did try. But I knew that my hands aren't made for this kind of work. Anyway, I tried really hard this time to get it right. When Mami finally nodded in approval, I got too excited and dipped the brush too far into the toilet, causing water to splash over us both.

"¡Ay! Ya déjalo. Está bien"—Enough! Leave it. Go!

Mami took the brush out of my hand and instructed me to get the mop. The one last step I intentionally forgot, and hoped Mami wouldn't notice, was mopping the floor. My least favorite chore of all. Maybe I hated mopping because I thought of mops as a cesspool of old water germs ready to infect me with diseases like the black plague or tuberculosis. Or was it that I found mopping illogical, like having to make my bed every day. I was going to go back to sleep in it later that night, so making the bed seemed like a waste of time and energy. I just didn't understand how submerging a stick with loose rope-like strands into a bucket of dirty Pine-Sol water over and over could actually clean anything. Or maybe it was because I was afraid that if I learned how to *"trapear el piso bien"* like Mami, that I'd be a slave to tiled and linoleum floors the rest of my life. Whatever the reason, I always "forgot" to mop and I always managed to get caught.

Nothing ever got past Mami, especially not anything related to house cleaning. If I didn't dust behind the television, she saw it from across the room and made me do it again. If I didn't vacuum underneath the bed, she lifted the comforter and could tell by the lack of vacuum cleaner lines that I had only done a half-ass job. If the bathroom or the kitchen hadn't been mopped and the floors were still sticky or stained or the countertops hadn't been wiped clean of stray water drops, I was called back to do it again.

Mami wasn't trying to be mean, she was just meticulous. And she came from a place where women took pride in the cleanliness and order of their homes. Mami grew up in the 1950s and '60s in the Dominican Republic, where a woman's best chance at life was marrying a respectable man, building a home together and bearing his children. *Una mujer decente* knew how to cook and clean and raise a baby by the age of twenty-five. Mami was only trying to prepare me to be a decent, respectable wife. But I rejected her expectations often, because I knew that in America, things were different. I knew that in the 90s, women had more options than to be somebody's wife and mother. I was getting an education like Papi wanted for me, so I could go to college and have a "real" job using my hands to write or educate or do something more meaningful. I was not going to be stuck at home serving other people, like Mami had been. And yet, back then, I didn't realize that what Mami was trying to teach me was meaningful. She was trying to teach me survival skills that I would need to have whether I got married or not. That using my hands to take care of myself, my house and my family was something to be proud of. But that was something I wouldn't come to understand until much later.

When I returned from the kitchen with the mop Mami filled a bucket with warm water and added about a half cup of citrus-scented Pine-Sol. She lifted and dunked the mop into the bucket like a plumber trying to unclog a toilet. The water swished and sloshed and splashed around in the bucket. Then she handed me the mop and told me to stand at the back of the bathroom near the toilet bowl. Then, she told me to turn around with my butt facing the door and to walk backwards moving the mop left to right. She said I had to walk backwards so I wouldn't leave my dirty footprints on the clean floor.

I did as instructed, but the mop was heavy, and my frail and flabby arms could not scrub the floor as hard as Mami wanted me to. I missed the area behind the toilet bowl and by the sink. But Mami let me finish. When I got to the bathroom door, my body in the hallway, Mami surveyed the tile and, without scorn, took the mop out of my hands, dunked it into the bucket a few more times and began to clean the entire floor herself.

I was riddled with guilt and disappointed in myself because, yet again, I realized that I was not good at the things Mami wanted me to be good at. I wanted Mami to be proud of me, but I was not talented in the art of housekeeping. Instead, I read thick books in English, like Papi did. I wrote short stories about twin sisters with brown hair and green eyes who wanted to sail around the world looking for buried treasure. I adapted fairytales and legends of the first Christmas with Santa Claus or the first Halloween into apocalyptic sci-fi tales of terror and destruction. Papi was always bringing home large green hardback ledgers from work for me to write in. I always filled them up in a few week's time. Papi encouraged my literary pursuits and enjoyed it when I read my stories aloud to him. Mami also knew that my education was important. She wanted me to do well in school, but I couldn't read her my stories because she didn't understand them. I wrote in English, and Mami only spoke Spanish. I knew that if she could just hear how creative I was, she'd let me spend my days reading and writing instead of dusting and scrubbing.

I wanted Mami to be proud of me. I knew that could only happen if I grew up to be *una mujer decente*, a decent woman who knew how to cook *arroz, habichuelas y carne*. A decent woman who set the table, washed the dishes and wiped down the counter tops. A decent woman who kept her home free of *cucarachas y microbios*. I was only eleven, but soon enough (I hoped), I'd get my period and become a *señorita,* and then Mami would see me as her equal (I believed). Then, we could have the American mother-daughter relationship I'd always wanted. I could tell her about my secret crushes, and she'd teach me to wear make-up. We'd shop and giggle, and she'd teach me everything I needed to know about being a woman. Those days would eventually come, later in my twenties and thirties. In fact, I would one day want nothing more than to be a good wife for my husband and would ask her what it was like to carry and mother a child because for me, doing so wouldn't come easy. But that was something I was not able to foresee at that age. So instead, in an effort to keep the peace, I sucked up my American dreams of what I assumed our relationship should be and accepted the Dominican version of my story.

I asked her what else I could do around the house to help. "Mami, *¿qué más necesitas?*" I shuffled my feet, and the words almost got caught in my throat, exposing my insincerity.

Mami paused in her meditative mopping and turned her head to look at me over her shoulder. She was sweating bullets and her hands were wrinkled like the skin of a spoiled *aguacate* from having wrung out the dirty mop one too many times. The bottom of her grey sweatpants were soaked with dirty Pine-Sol water. She wiped her brow with the sleeve of her hair-dye-stained T-shirt. I felt bad for Mami, working and sweating and breaking her back while Papi read on the couch and my brother and sister played video games or ran around outside. I wanted to be of use, but I really hated doing chores. I wished I could help in some other way, but I couldn't figure out how. I could read to her in Spanish while she cleaned. But my Spanish reading skills weren't very good. Perhaps if I just stayed out of her way, like my brother and sister did, that would be more helpful. But I knew that was not an option, I was the eldest daughter, I was expected to help. Instead, I gave up on finding a non-cleaning way of helping and waited for her orders.

Mami stared at my defeated face and knew that once again the cleanliness, or pride, of the home was dependent solely on her. She returned to the task at hand without saying a word. I watched her shoulder blades glide closer to her spine as her chest lifted and she put her hand on her hip as if holding onto a pain that refused to let go. She lifted her head up to the ceiling as if asking God for some relief and she sighed in resignation.

"*Nada*," she said, "*no me puedes ayudar en más nada. Yo termino.*"—Nothing, you can't help me with anything. I'll finish.

I lowered my head and walked back to my room in silence. I didn't know if I'd ever make her proud or if she would ever value the same things I did. I wanted us to find some common ground, but it seemed like we were from two different worlds, and our islands kept drifting farther and farther apart. I swallowed my frustration, knowing there was no one I could talk to about any of it. I found my most recent copy of *The Babysitter's Club*, and went to my room, where I knew I could get lost in a world of words.

Jasminne, age 1,
in Alabama.

Jasminne, age 6,
posing for her first-
grade school photo
in Louisiana.

Jasminne, age 7, in First Communion attire in Fort Polk.

Jasminne, age 7, at her grandmother's house in New York.

Jasminne, age 9, her brother Ben, age 11, and her sister Jennifer, age 5, on Easter Sunday in Germany.

Jasminne, age 10, with Mom (Sonia) and her sister Jennifer at Disney World.

Jasminne, age 14, before a band concert when she was a freshman in high school, San Antonio, Texas.

Jasminne, age 17, at her high school graduation with her parents (Benjamin and Sonia), San Antonio, Texas.

A Polaroid Picture

In the Polaroid picture Mami keeps on her antique dresser, my baby cousin Nicholas is sleeping. When I stop to really look at him in the picture, I trace his face and his body with my hands. I brush my fingertips along his soft purplish cheeks filled with toothless gums, his round button nose that never inhaled his mother's skin and his small gentle lips that never opened to drink his mother's breast milk, take a sip of water, say a first word or stretch to form a smile. He rests softly in a blue and white fleece receiving blanket and his little fists and feet are wrapped in socks and mittens. When I look at his photo, I really do like to pretend he's just sleeping.

Tía María was about six months pregnant when she and my two other aunts, Carmen and Milagro, my uncle Fernando and my grandmother got their "papers" to come to the United States to live with us. They weren't moving to New York, like so many Dominican immigrants did. My parents were bringing them to Clarksville, Tennessee, a small southern town where the population of Dominicans would now sky-rocket because of their arrival.

As a child who had never been so close to a pregnant woman before, I found her protruding belly and her slow waddle fascinating. What I didn't expect was that my first experience with pregnancy would also be my first experience with death.

Mami and Papi were busy before my relatives' arrival organizing papers, rearranging furniture and emptying closets. They ran errands around town to the bank, the post office, the notary and the grocery store. There was going to be a lot more mouths to feed, and Mami wanted no one to go hungry, because *"en América nadie se muere de hambre"*—no one goes hungry in the United States. Papi and Ben arranged a couple of queen-sized beds in the family den of our seventies-style split-level house and set up a dresser along one of the wood-paneled walls. That was where my extended family would sleep and live. Mami explained that the arrangement was more luxurious and comfortable than the tiny cement and dirt houses they were used to on the island.

Mami was the oldest female of the ten children my grandparents had: a total of five girls and five boys. I don't know the exact order of all the boys and girls in the middle, but I do know that because Mami was the oldest daughter (like me), she was responsible for taking care of the house and raising her siblings. Perhaps this is why she felt compelled to do the hard work of getting them all "papers" and bringing them stateside.

On the day of their arrival, we woke up early, took showers and got dressed. Mami began cooking rice, beans and *carne guisada* early. She wanted to leave everything ready so that when they arrived from the airport, they would sit and have a warm, home-cooked meal. Mami and Papi left in the mid-afternoon to the Nashville airport to pick everyone up. As latchkey kids our whole lives, my siblings and I were used to being home alone for hours at a time. The drive from Clarksville to Nashville was at least an hour each way, so I knew it would be some time before they arrived. I busied myself with toys and TV and books for about an hour before I grew restless and bored. Once I thought almost two hours had passed, I set the table, as Mami had instructed, and then I kneeled on the couch, opened the curtain, stared out the window and waited.

When they pulled up to the driveway, I yelled to Ben and Jenny, "They're here! They're here!"

I rushed outside to help with their suitcases and bags, since I knew Mami would ask me to anyway. As everyone got out of the minivan and entered the house, Mami told me to ask my grandmother, my aunts and my uncle for their blessing. It was the only proper way for me to greet my elders.

"*Bésale la mano a Mamá y a tus tías y a tu tío,*" Mami said, asking me to kiss them. I hugged them all, gave each a peck on the cheek and greeted them properly.

"*Bendición, Mamá. Bendición, Tía. Bendición, Tía. Bendición, Tía. Bendición, Tío.*"

I smiled wide, and they marveled at how much I had grown from the pictures Mami had sent over a year ago. Then they took all of their belongings, which I found to be scarce, considering they had packed up "their whole lives" to start anew, to the downstairs den where they would be living.

Papi invited my uncle Fernando upstairs to the kitchen for a beer and left the five women (Mami included), all under five feet tall, to put away all of their things. Like a tribe of ants whose hill had just been kicked over, these women scurried about the room setting bags down, picking bags up, shaking out bed sheets, fluffing pillows and talking so loud and so quickly anyone not from the island would assume they were bickering. Their Spanish was quick and short. Most of the sounds at the end of their sentences were cut off, as if they just had too much to say and not enough time. Words like "está" became "ta;" "para acá" became "pa'cá;" and phrases like "es que tú no sabes" became "e' que tú no sabe" or "hazme el favor" became "ha' me 'l favor." Their dialogue was non-linear, boisterous, sarcastic and witty. Half the time you weren't sure to whom you were supposed to be listening to or responding. It was like playing a game of auditory ping-pong. Back and forth you entered and exited conversations mid-sentence, speaking louder than the person before you.

As they set their things down and gabbed away about the children, spouses, cousins and neighbors they left behind, I stood in the doorway and absorbed their shapes, their smells and the sounds of their island tongue. Carmen, the *tía* I had met before looked exactly as she had the last time I saw her. She was short and had wavy auburn hair. Her skin was caramel-colored with a hint of mustard near the cheeks and under the eyes. She had skinny legs and a large bust that seemed to be playing tug of war with the buttons on her ruby-red silk blouse. She was the loudest of all my aunts and always seemed the happiest. Tía Milagro and Tía María were the shortest of the sisters, probably no more than 4'8" each. They both had thick thighs, wide childbearing hips and strong but worn hands like Mami's that were prepared for hard labor and a lot of praying. At the time, I wanted to assume María was pregnant, since her belly stuck out more than the others, but I knew asking her would be impolite. So I waited until one of the adults brought it up or I "accidentally" overheard it in conversation.

After the commotion of settling in subsided, we all went upstairs to eat. There, they continued sharing gossip about my great aunts and their children who'd had kids out of wedlock, my uncles and their ungrateful wives, neighbors who had converted from Catholicism to Seventh Day Adventists and acquaintances whose daughters were out-of-control, among other juicy topics.

After dinner, Tía María grabbed her belly and burped. Everyone laughed and asked her if she and the baby were okay. There. My suspicions had been confirmed. This new revelation made their arrival twice as exciting. Soon a baby would be arriving too, and I wanted to know so many things about this unborn child, but I kept my mouth shut because I knew asking an adult questions was rude.

When my siblings and I were done eating, we were told to go play or watch TV. I knew this was code for "the adults have important things to discuss." And as much as I hated to leave their conversation, I cleared my plate and went to my room. I don't know what they discussed the rest of that night as I went to bed to the sound of laughter, "shushing," Papi's bad jokes and the clinking and clanking of plates and cups. I assume Mami and Papi had to talk to them about finding jobs and figuring out transportation and just what it was like to live in the United States, specifically how different Clarksville, Tennessee was to Santo Domingo.

"American lifestyle is different than life on the island," I could imagine Papi saying. "It's not easy, especially for you, since you don't know the language. Things will be hard at first, and you'll have to be willing to take whatever job you can get: washing dishes, factory work, cleaning toilets . . . anything at all. You'll have to work hard, and it will take time, but it will be worth it."

About three months after they arrived, Tía María started having stomach pains in the middle of the night. She would wake up and pace the downstairs hallway, moaning and breathing heavily. She'd call for Mami several times before my mom would get up and go down to her. I too would get up and walk to the end of the upstairs hallway, where I'd stare down the staircase, trying to understand what all the commotion was about. Mami would have her arm around María and rub her belly. Maria would keep repeating that she was in pain.

Then one night, Mami told her to sit down and not move. Mami came upstairs, told me to go back to bed and told Papi to get dressed. They were going to take María to the hospital. I heard drawers and doors open and close. I heard my aunts whispering in the living room. Then I heard the garage door open, the engine rev up and the car drive off. I laid in bed with my eyes wide open, eagerly awaiting the arrival of my baby cousin. I wondered what he would look like, if Mami would let me hold him, if he would be soft and warm and perfect in every way. Everyone had assumed it was going to be a boy, because María's hair was long and shiny and because the shape of her stomach sat to the left just so. I didn't know what any of those superstitious signs meant, but that night I thought about him eagerly until my eyes grew heavy and I fell back asleep.

A few hours later, they returned. I heard the garage door open, and Mami, Papi and María entered the house. There was rustling and talking downstairs. I heard several footsteps walking up the stairs. I wanted to rush out of my room to greet the new baby. I had no idea how long it took to birth a child and I assumed that if they were back already that meant the baby had arrived. But because it was the middle of the night and I knew I would get yelled at for not being in bed, I stayed in my room and tried to listen to what Mami was saying to someone out in the hallway.

I heard one of my *tías* ask what happened. Mami told her that none of the doctors at the hospital emergency room would see her because she didn't have insurance and she didn't have any medical records. They waited as long as they could, and when they told her that she wasn't in labor and they couldn't give her anything anyway, they decided to come home and rest. My little heart weighed heavy, and I almost cried. I was so disappointed that we didn't have a baby in the house yet. I didn't want my *tía* to be in pain, but more than anything I wanted to see my new baby cousin.

The next day Mami and Papi went to work, I went to school and María stayed in bed. My other *tías* took care of her and tried to keep her comfortable. That night after dinner, she said her pains had gotten worse and that she was sure she was also having contractions and going into labor. María had been pregnant twice before with the two children she had left behind in the DR, so she knew what was happening. Mami and Papi helped get her into the car and rushed her to the hospital. The rest of the family tried to busy themselves by reading the Bible, praying, pacing, cooking and cleaning. For almost thirty-six hours I didn't see Mami or Papi. The phone rang a couple of times, and I heard my aunts whispering over the phone.

Then a call came in and caused Carmen, Milagro and my grandmother to burst into uncontrollable sobs. I stood in the doorway of the kitchen and watched them embrace each other, their chests heaving, their voices murmuring the Our Father. When my grandmother noticed me, she told me to go watch TV. She said Mami and Papi would be home soon and there was nothing I needed to worry about, that all of this was adult stuff: "*cosas de adultos.*" I complied and sat down sullen on the couch.

After about an episode and a half of *Family Matters* on the TV, I heard the car pull into the driveway. Mami and Papi came in and went to the kitchen. I wondered where María and the baby were. No one said a word. Papi opened the fridge and took out two beers. He gave one to my uncle, and I heard them pop the bottle caps. Mami and the other women whispered in between sobs. I was too afraid to go into the kitchen, so I waited for something, anything to happen in the living room. Finally, what seemed like an eternity later, Mami and Papi called my siblings and me into their bedroom.

We all crawled into their queen-sized bed and listened to what they had to say. Papi explained in very deliberate and medical terms that María's baby was stillborn. She'd had a C-section, that revealed the baby's

umbilical cord had wrapped around its neck. He was
dead even before they arrived at the hospital. I heard his
words, but as a child it didn't make sense to me. How
could a baby be dead before it was even born? Didn't
they try to revive him? Where was my aunt? Was she
dead too? All these questions swirled around in my
head, but I couldn't find the right words in Spanish to
ask them. And then, because I guess Mami had run out
of words too, she simply placed a 3.5 x 4 Polaroid picture of the sleeping baby on the bed and told us my aunt
had named him Nicholas, like his father.

I shoved my face into a pillow and wept. Mami
rubbed my back and told me to relax. I felt the warmth
of her hand on my back, but it sent chills down my
spine. I shivered and held the pillow close. Mami said
María was still in the hospital recovering but she would
be home tomorrow. She said she understood that it was
a hard time for all of us, but the important thing was that
we were a family. María would need time to rest, she
added, and she and Papi would take care of the funeral
arrangements. In the meantime, the best thing we could
do was stay out of the way and not make much noise.

For the next few days, the grief I felt in my tiny ten-
year-old body made me slouch and drag my feet. The
joy and anticipation I had felt only days earlier turned
to sorrow. I didn't know how to process my emotions,
and there was no one I could talk to. Mami and Papi
were busy preparing the funeral, Ben immersed himself
in video games and Jenny was too small to really understand what was happening. I considered resurrecting
my imaginary friend Linda in order to feel less alone,
but I couldn't imagine what we'd talk about now.

Finally, in an effort to "make myself scarce" and
occupy my mind, I decided to pick out funeral outfits
for Jenny and me. We were going to go to our first
funeral. I wanted to be sure we showed respect by wearing appropriate attire. I spent the better part of the day
taking out every piece of black clothing Jenny and I
owned. I placed them neatly on our shared bed, and she
and I practiced our own private fashion show.

We tried on dresses, blouses and skirts, pants, a vest,
sweaters and tank tops. I had to make sure the skirts or
dresses we wore weren't too short. We had to wear
sleeves, because Papi didn't like us showing our arms.
Besides, it was getting cold. I don't remember what the
exact outfits were we decided on, but I know I was
proud of myself for figuring it out so Mami wouldn't
have to. I knew she would be relieved that we were
being so independent.

I set the outfits on a chair in our bedroom and just
waited for the moment when Mami would tell me to get
ready. Two days passed, and I kept waiting. Mami and
Papi rushed about the house, made phone calls and
cooked enough food to feed twice the amount of people
living with us. They had brought María home the day
after they told us the news, but I had only seen her
once. She walked slowly, holding herself up against the
wall and looking like she'd been punched in both eyes.

She didn't say anything to me, but I greeted her and
said, "*Bendición, Tía.*"

She looked at me but couldn't manage a smile. Mami
helped her to the bed, and that was where she stayed
until the day of the funeral.

On the morning of the fifth day after my "fashion show," I heard everyone moving about in a frenzy. The shower kept turning on and off, and my aunts' voices started to get louder and louder. I went to Mami's room to find out what was going on. She was dressed in black and putting on make-up. My heart jumped. Today was the funeral. I was finally going to get to go to a funeral!

Mami stopped applying her soft pink rouge and looked at me through the reflection in the mirror.

"Today is the funeral. All of the adults will attend. But you, your brother and sister will stay at home with a babysitter." She said it matter-of-factly, as if she had just told me to set the table. Then she picked the brush back up and finished applying the rouge. The incomprehensible grief I had felt just a few days before rushed over my body again and gave me goose bumps. My shoulders hunched and I shuffled my feet in frustration. I wanted to challenge Mami and explain that Jenny and I already had our outfits picked out and everything. I wanted to tell her that we would be good little Dominican girls and stay quiet and be nice and greet everyone properly. I wanted to tell her that I had never been to a funeral before and that I really wanted to go.

Then my eyes found hers in the mirror. She looked down at the Polaroid of my dead baby cousin tucked in a corner of the mirror on her dresser. She looked at it for only a moment and then kept applying her make-up. My eyes were held captive. His eyes were closed, but I felt him looking at me. He was trying to tell me something with his stillness. His ashen cocoa-colored face reminded me that Mami had enough to deal with already. Now was not the time to try to get my way.

Nicholas was asking me to just let it go. Let him go. Although I wanted nothing more than to cry and throw a tantrum, I let the tears in my eyes fall back into their sockets. I silently left the room.

I put my outfit back in the closet and waited until all the adults had left the house before leaving my room. When I walked over to Mami's bedroom, the voices that normally filled the corners of each room had fallen silent. The house felt heavier, and I was afraid the walls would start to close in on me at any moment. I didn't want to be alone. I felt uneasy with the way my footsteps echoed in the hall.

I had tiptoed my way over to my mom's dresser and picked up the Polaroid. It felt sterile and cold in my hands. It was not at all what I had expected to feel while holding a newborn. As I looked closely at the picture, I noticed that he wasn't lying on a bed or in a crib, as I had originally thought. Someone was holding him. I presumed it was my aunt, but her face was not in the photo. All I could see was a single dark-brown tired hand gripping the baby's bottom.

The picture itself was glossy, and his blue and white onesie and blanket were vibrant in the photo. His face was not. Baby Nicholas looked like a hollow, deflated balloon. As I turned the picture left and right, up and down, trying to see him for the three-dimensional being he was, I decided that this Polaroid picture would never be enough to keep this baby alive, now or ever.

Respect Your Elders

One noisy and family-filled Sunday afternoon, during my rebellious middle school years when I hated everything about my life and my family, I sat on the couch with my maternal grandmother, watching television and wishing I were somewhere else. I wanted to be outside, walking around with my friends or at the mall trying on clothes I couldn't afford. Mami had forbidden me from locking myself up in my room as usual, so I had plopped myself on the couch in front of the TV next to my *abuela*, the only person I knew wouldn't try to talk to me about their problems. She was sipping some *café con leche* and eating flan, which she should not have because of her Type II diabetes and high cholesterol. I wanted to admonish her, the way I'd seen Mami do behind her back. But she was one of our elders, and I knew better than to try and argue with her. Abuela was from an era that made her stubborn enough to do whatever she wanted. She grew up during the time of the fierce Dominican dictator, Rafael Leonidas Trujillo, when respect was gained by imposing fear and absolute rule and when no one questioned authority.

As I watched her sip her coffee and spoon flan into her dentured mouth, I shook my head silently, wondering how she had made it that far in life. She asked me to bring her a glass of water even though she already had coffee. I grunted and got up, annoyed at the fact that I was never left alone any more and was always being required to serve others.

Abuela was in her sixties and had made a career out of being served by others. She had never worked a day in her life, from what Mami had told me, and the only type of labor she understood was in childbirth, which she had accomplished twelve times. Mami had said that back in Santo Domingo she had occasionally sewn clothes for some of the women in town, but that was only if times were really tough and my now-deceased paternal grandfather couldn't provide for her and all the children. Mostly though, Abuela got Mami to raise the rest of the children and to serve her hand and foot. Mami cooked and cleaned for all of us, took Abuela to the doctor and picked up her meds, helped her with her insulin, paid for her trips back to the DR every six months, drove her to the store when she was feeling restless and wanted to window shop, and took her to the salon to get her hair relaxed and dyed. Abuela, who insisted she was of Spanish and Taíno Native American blood only, was a "light-skinned" Dominican with mostly "good hair" that she relaxed only because of its minor kink.

When I returned with her glass of water, I studied her salt and pepper hair, which rested straight and flat with a slight flip at the nape of her neck. It was shiny from the oil she slathered on it daily to keep it from frizzing. I could tell by the greys near her scalp that she was due for a touch up. I handed her the glass of water, and she gulped it down, complaining about the American summer heat being more miserable than the heat on the island. She wiped her chin with the fabric from her long, blue floral skirt. She handed back to me the glass and continued savoring her flan, her hands trembling with each bite, the fork clinking against Mami's fake China.

The television was playing a rerun of some Latino music award show, but I had learned to tune out the white noise on days like these, days when we had come together as a family to celebrate one more birthday or anniversary or fallen tooth. They were days when the whole family would be in the kitchen talking loudly. Something would be frying on the stove, and my baby cousins would scurry around and knock over drinks and plates of food. The radio and the television would hum incessantly in the background while people laughed and orders were shouted at the children.

Abuela was staring at the TV intently, trying to make sense of all that she was watching but could not hear. A tall woman with beautiful voluptuous curls and dark ebony skin came on the screen, wearing an emerald low-cut gown that hugged her hips and waist like labels on a Coke bottle. She began to sing a soulful ballad. Abuela was entranced.

"Where is she from?" Abuela asked me.

"I don't know, but she's beautiful *¿no crees?*"

"Yes, she's beautiful," Abuela agreed, "but you know, that dark skin, she looks *Haitian."* The word fell out of her mouth like a disease, as if she was swatting at a pesky fruit fly with her tongue.

"And you know," she continued, "it doesn't matter what *they* do, those Haitians, you know they have that *smell.*" She shook her head disapprovingly, her nose wrinkled and she took another sip of her *café*.

I shifted my weight on the couch, wanting to defend the woman on TV, but I didn't know how. I wanted to tell my grandmother that she was being racist and rude, that it was wrong to say those things. But I didn't know how to say anything without being disrespectful. So I kept my mouth shut and waited for her to say something to redeem herself.

She just kept studying the woman on the screen and, without noticing the appalled look on my face, she continued, "She's beautiful, but it won't matter how hard she scrubs, she'll still have that smell, you know? . . . that *Haitian* smell. You just can't get rid of that smell, you know?"

I didn't know what smell Abuela was talking about. I had never met anyone from Haiti before, but I had heard things like this from other family members before. I knew that Dominicans had a history of discriminating against and distrusting Haitians. Even though I didn't know where it came from, I knew a part of it had to do with how light or dark their skin was. I still couldn't understand Abuela's disgust with this assumed Haitian woman on TV, however. After all, my late grandfather was just as dark as this woman was. Had she not married him and had his children, some who were also just as dark-skinned as this singer? And my own father and brother *could* be Haitian, if they were judged only by their skin color. Did that mean she felt disgust towards them too? I got up from the couch, too flustered to sit still, but too young and ignorant to articulate my thoughts in a meaningful way. I wanted to tell her she was wrong and that she shouldn't talk about Haitians or anyone that way. I wanted to change her mind about how she felt about an entire group of people. But instead, I simply took her now empty cup and plate away and said, "*Ay, Abuela* . . ." I rushed to leave the room to avoid anymore of her disdain. I left her alone with the TV in the living room and let her words dissolve into the *bachata* playing on the radio and into the sizzle of *plátanos* frying on the stove. I tried to convince myself that Abuela was from a different era and her way of thinking was not her fault.

THE TALK

"*Siéntate ahí, que te voy a decir algo*"—sit down, we need to tell you something—was the way both Mami and Papi would start any serious conversation with my siblings and me.

These talks could involve anything from why we earned a C on our report cards to why we had lied about where we were the previous night. On occasion, when I hadn't done anything wrong or broken one of their rules to warrant a scolding, these talks were about life lessons or well-crafted, subtle apologies for something my parents felt remorseful about. Sometimes Papi wanted to explain why he was so strict with me about earning good grades. Other times Mami wanted me to understand that she was not an American mother and that, no matter how hard I begged, I wouldn't be allowed to shave my legs, wear make-up, wax my eyebrows or buy heels until I was fifteen—end of story.

But to my dismay, or perhaps to my benefit depending on how you look at it, there were two talks I never got from Mami and Papi: the sex talk and the period talk. The sex talk wasn't really necessary because what was expected of us was always implied: Sex leads to babies. Sex is bad. Don't do it until you're married. The

dire consequences and shame of having sex always
came up in adult conversations I eavesdropped on. Papi
would say, talking about my sister and me, "If either of
them ever finds out she's pregnant while living under
MY roof, she better not even bother coming home." And
anytime Mami would find out one of her cousin's teen
daughters had ended up "*con un domingo siete,*" pregnant out of wedlock, she would just suck her teeth and
repeat "*qué lástima,*" what a shame. I knew teen pregnancy was shameful and unforgivable in my house. I
had no interest in being homeless or disowned, so I
knew all I needed to know about having sex: it wasn't
for me.

The period talk, however, was something I really was
looking forward to but never got. In fifth grade, Mami
was asked to sign a permission slip allowing the school
to have a talk with me about hygiene and puberty.
Because Mami didn't speak or read English, she usually
signed all papers that came home, regardless of what
they said as long as I could give her a vague explanation
of what she was signing. In this case, I told her that
someone was going to talk to us about using deodorant
because we were starting to smell.

The truth was, for two days the entire fifth grade
class was divided into a girl's only room and a boy's only
room. Those students whose parents hadn't signed the
form were taken to the library to do busy work and read
all day. During those two days, a professional did come
and talk to us about hygiene and deodorant, but she
also spent about two hours showing us a video and
reading through a pamphlet about menstruation. The
pamphlet was really cute and looked like the cover of

Seventeen Magazine. It was pink and purple with three smiling girls on the front: a white girl with blond hair and blue eyes, an Asian girl with a bob and a black girl with a side ponytail. They all looked very excited to be on their periods at a sunny park with blooming flowers and a large fountain in the background, which made me believe going through puberty would be pleasant and easy.

The two-day seminar consisted of reading through the pamphlet titled, "The Changes In Your Body," which included growing breasts, growth spurts, oily skin and pimples and, of course, your first period and cramps. We then learned how to keep track of our cycles using a calendar and a red pen. We watched a video of an egg being released from an ovary. We were also engaged with a hands-on display of maxi pads, with and without wings, tampons with and without applicators, panty liners, feminine wipes and yeast infection creams. Afterwards, we were allowed to ask questions, but I was too shy. Instead, I let myself be consumed by the jovial pamphlet that I was allowed to take home.

I was only ten then, but I was ready and excited to get my first period and to grow breasts. Anytime I felt something weird "down there," I'd go back and reread the pamphlet. I wanted to know everything I could before starting my period. And I really hoped that Mami would add to that knowledge one day. I never considered that perhaps she didn't want to because it meant that her little girl was growing up. Or that perhaps her own mother had never had "the period talk" with her and she just didn't realize it was something she had to do.

In the meantime, I relied on the words in that ten-page booklet. I flipped through and read that pamphlet a hundred times for the next several years. When it wasn't in my backpack, I kept it hidden in the shoebox on the top shelf of my closet, where I kept all my hidden treasures, notes and letters. I didn't want Mami to find it and think it was trash and throw it away. I preserved that little booklet like it was the original Holy Bible.

Before that class, the only thing I knew about getting your period, which I also only learned by chance, was that once you got it, you were a "*señorita*." I also learned, by listening in on conversations between my mom and her sisters, that Mami didn't become a *señorita* until she was sixteen. Sixteen?! I couldn't wait that long! I was ready to become a señorita then and there. I wanted it because everyone made it seem like being a señorita meant you earned certain privileges. These privileges included sitting with the other women at dinners and birthday parties to talk about women things, like clothes and men and other women and how spoiled the children were. I assumed it meant I could shave, pluck my unibrow, wear make-up, heels and shorter skirts. I believed it meant that Mami wouldn't see me as a kid anymore, which is what I wanted and what she feared. I thought that being a *señorita* meant I would soon have a seat at the grown-up table and everyone would start to treat me like the adult I always felt I was. But I realized later that's not what it meant at all.

I got my first period three months after my thirteenth birthday, on February 10, 1997. I remember the date because it was a Monday morning and we had just celebrated my parent's wedding anniversary over the weekend. I knew my period would be coming soon, because over the last three years, after the fifth-grade talk at school, my breasts had sprouted and I kept running them into things. I also had grown taller from about 4'8" to 5'1." I also had more of an interest in boys, beyond trying to beat them at tetherball. Also, my leg and underarm hair was thicker and more embarrassing now.

Despite Mami's protestations and Papi's rules about not shaving or removing any body hair until my fifteenth birthday, I had shaved my underarms at eleven because I believed they were contributing to my bad odor. I also began to shave my legs shortly after my thirteenth birthday because I was being bullied during gym by the other eighth graders. They called me names like "Wolfie" and "Cousin It," and the boys would taunt me by saying, "You have more hair on your legs than I do on my head!" I was one of the only girls that still hadn't shaved her legs, and those that hadn't yet, didn't need to because they were blondes and you couldn't see it anyway.

My body hair, on the other hand, was thick and black and it was everywhere. It seemed as if the hair on my head decided to cross all my body's borders and colonize every inch of it, regardless of what I wanted. As I entered puberty, the hair on my scalp began by covering the edge of my face and connecting with my eyebrows. It then crept over into my sideburns, reached down the back of my ear and behind my neck, trailed over to my shoulders, arms, underarms, forearms and wrists. It was on the back of my neck, in a happy trail from my breastbone down to my belly button and stomach until it found its way all around my vagina. My pubic hair formed a pact with the wiry hairs on my thighs and became one until it softened a bit on my knees, straightened and then grew as dense and as quickly as a chia pet on my calves. The only place I didn't have hair was on my palms and the bottom of my feet. Even my knuckles and toes had hair!

All this unwanted hair made me feel dirty and ugly. I was tired of wearing sweatpants while everyone else wore gym shorts and cute tank tops. It was the late nineties, and short plaid skirts were all the rage. I hated wearing dark tights to hide my legs all the time. So I decided I would break the cardinal rule of not shaving, regardless of whatever consequence came, because the kids at school were meaner than Mami or Papi could ever be. I was tired of it. I started by shaving only my ankles at first, since I knew I could hide them by wearing socks. At first I just wanted to see what my legs would look like without hair. And it was everything I'd hoped. My legs looked lighter, cleaner, smoother and more beautiful. I could see my caramel skin and I could rub my hands across my ankles the way the women did in Gillette razor commercials. After Mami didn't notice that I shaved my ankles, I was brave enough to shave my calves. I borrowed one of Papi's dark blue disposable Gillette razors after school one day while they were still at work and I shaved both my legs to the knee. I then covered them in lotion, which stung, since I had numerous nicks and cuts. I kept staring at them in my room. When I heard the garage door open, I quickly threw on some pants.

I didn't wear skirts or dresses around Mami and Papi for a couple of weeks. I knew Mami had noticed because she did a double take once while we were at church. We were sitting in the pew during the last song as the priest and altar boys were walking down the aisle. She leaned over to pick up her purse and noticed my legs. Clutching her purse in her hands, she looked at me up and down and said very quietly in Spanish, "You think I didn't notice that you shaved your legs, but I did. I did notice." And then between her teeth she pointed at me and said, "I am keeping score, all of these little things you keep doing, that you think you are getting away with. I am keeping score." This meant that down the road she might punish me for all of them all at once. I couldn't look her in the eye then. I played with the hem of my skirt and felt the heat rise in my cheeks. It was bad enough that she had actually found me out, but it was even worse that she chose to admonish me at church, in front of Jesus.

At that moment, however, I just thanked God that she had kept our secret from Papi, who would've actually punished me on the spot. I also know now, that all of these rules weren't because they hated me (like I assumed then), but because they were trying to preserve my childhood. They didn't want me to lose my innocence, to run away from home and become a *cualquiera*, a no-named woman with poor values and no self-respect. But, some of their rules, to my American self, were just too arbitrary and frustrating to follow. So I broke them. I broke them to fit in, to feel beautiful and maybe one day to be popular.

On the day I got my first period, I wasn't thinking about body hair or Mami or fitting in or being popular. I was still daydreaming about my first crush, Juan, a

Puerto Rican boy who was a year younger than me and
whose mother worked with my mom at the daycare cen-
ter on base. He had light brown skin, thick brown wavy
hair and dimples. He didn't go to my school because his
family lived on base, but we saw each other often at
family dinner parties, birthdays, holiday celebrations
and occasionally at Mass on Sundays.

I woke up the morning of my first period smiling
and ready to start the day. I had seen Juan at a get-
together at my godmother's house the previous night.
Although he spent most of the time playing video games
with my brother, I liked being able to sit in the same
room with him and talk to him whenever he would
pause the game long enough to listen.

I got up that next day and went to the bathroom to
brush my teeth and get ready for school. I peed and
wiped and looked at the toilet paper before flushing
it away. Right there on the paper was a big glob of red-
dish-brown sludge. My heart skipped a beat. It was happening! My period was happening, I was officially a
señorita!

"Maaaa! Maaaa!" I yelled out while still sitting on
the toilet with the paper in my hands and my under-
wear around my ankles.

Mami came rushing in, all worried. "*¿Qué pasó?*"

I showed her the toilet paper in my hands.

She looked down at it, then back up at me. Her face
was expressionless. She said, "Okay," and told me to
flush the paper away. Then she said, "Hold on," and
dashed out of the bathroom.

I sat on the toilet and waited.

A few minutes went by before she came back to the bathroom and handed me a thick pad. "*Toma. Avanza, que se te va a hacer tarde*"—Here, and hurry, 'cause it's getting late. She turned around and again left me alone in the bathroom.

My stomach cramped and all the joy of that moment was gone. I put the pad on, got off the toilet and took a long look in the mirror. I was hoping to see something, anything that showed I had become a woman. But as far as I could tell, I looked exactly the same. My hair was still frizzed, my skin was still oily and I hadn't grown any taller. I didn't even feel any prettier.

The only thing special about that day was that I was cursed with piercing cramps that felt like my stomach was wrestling with itself and losing. I dragged the weight of a twenty-pound rock around in my gut and felt so fatigued I even fell asleep in class. When I did have the energy to do anything, it was only to go to the bathroom. I spent half of that school day on the toilet holding my stomach, groaning and afraid that I was bleeding to death. No one had prepared me for the blood. Pad after pad was soaked, and it was not the pretty bright red blood you get from a cut. This blood was thick and different shades: ruby red, scarlet, crimson. I remember reading that this could last three to five days or even longer, and I didn't know if I would survive that long. The smiling girls on the cover of the pamphlet had made menstruation and puberty look so easy and like so much fun. But I was having a miserable time and I felt completely betrayed. Betrayed by my body, by my teachers, by the world that had not prepared me for any of this. Near the end of the school day, I went to the bathroom one last time and just sat on the floor and cried. Maybe it was from the pain. Maybe it was from the fatigue. Maybe it was from the disappointment of realizing that this wasn't the way I thought any of this would happen. I sobbed, wondering why I ever wanted to become a *señorita* in the first place. Maybe it was because the moment when I told Mami the news felt especially anti-climactic. Mami didn't hug me, or smile, or scream, or run off to call my *tías* and her girlfriends to tell them the good news. There was no day off from school to celebrate my transition. No special talk or tender moment between mother and daughter about womanhood. No new privileges earned.

This Monday turned out to be just like every other Monday, except instead of just handing me my lunch money before I left, Mami shoved three maxi pads in my backpack and told me to change it every three to four hours. Maybe Mami was too stunned and sad to be happy for me. Maybe she knew I was growing up and it was all happening too fast for her. Maybe she felt fear because she knew what the world could do to a woman. Maybe she spent that day cleaning and crying and mourning the end of my childhood. I know she felt *something* for me that day. Whatever it was, I'd like to believe she didn't say it because she didn't have the words yet. After all, I was her first daughter, and this was her first experience with my first period too.

PHENOMENAL WOMAN

Shortly after my first period, Papi took my siblings and me to a poetry reading by Maya Angelou. He was attending classes at Austin Peay State University in Clarksville, Tennessee and had reserved enough tickets for the four of us to attend. Mami stayed at home because she said she wouldn't understand what was happening, anyway, and at least this way she could clean the house without interruptions.

I had read some of Maya Angelou's poems in my English classes at school during Black History Month and I was excited to see her. I didn't realize how important and famous she was until we arrived at the university and the car line just to get into the parking lot was wrapped around the block. People honked their horns, traffic was stalled and I was worried we would miss the whole event.

"Papi, how much longer?" I asked as I tugged at my seatbelt and looked out the car window.

"Soon. We're almost there. Be patient. They won't start as long as all these people are still out here. Don't worry."

He was right. The event started almost forty-five minutes late. We slowly inched forward every couple of minutes and eventually made it into the lot. We found parking and had to walk what seemed like over a mile just to get into the auditorium. We climbed the almost three flights of stairs up to our seats and sat down. I looked out into the audience. There must have been at least three hundred people there, murmuring and rustling in their seats, presumably as excited as I was to see this icon of American literature read her poems and inspire us with her words.

I didn't have the greatest view of the stage because I was short and there was a large pillar blocking my sight line. I had asked my brother Ben to switch seats, but he was an even more avid reader of poetry than I was and was not willing to move.

As we settled into our seats, the lights dimmed and an older gentleman came to the podium. He welcomed everyone and introduced Ms. Angelou by reading her biography and asking us all to stand and welcome her with a round of applause. We did. When Maya Angelou came out to the podium, the auditorium shook. People clapped, whistled and some even stomped their feet. I hopped up and down like the giddy schoolgirl I was. Even though we were in the far back of the room, I had never been that close to a real-life published author before. I loved reading and writing so much that writers to me were like movie stars. I believed that they lived glamorous lives in big mansions reading fan mail, drinking coffee by a fireplace and autographing copies of their books all day. The way that room roared that night made me believe my assumptions were right.

Although I had always admired her work, I fell in love with her that night. She wore black pants, a soft black blouse, big gold hoop earrings, a long gold neck-lace and a head wrap. The only make-up she seemed to be wearing was bold-red lipstick. Her look was sleek and simple, but her voice vibrated our seats and her presence filled the room with magic. We were all capti-vated by the low hum of her vowels when she spoke, and no one dared make a sound or even breathe as she turned the pages of her book and read one poem after another. She spoke as if she were singing or praying to a loved one and she enjoyed laughing at her own quirks. She read poems I don't remember the names of now and poems like "Still I Rise" that to this day I carry in my bag.

I wanted to take Maya Angelou home with me that night. I didn't want just her words on the page to keep me company. I wanted her and her voice to reassure me whenever I felt like my life was too hard or Mami didn't understand me. Maya Angelou was the phenomenal woman I needed to be one day. It seemed, at the time, that she understood me better than anyone else. I heard my story in her story. I read my life in the stories and poems about her life. I knew that if Maya Angelou had overcome the challenges she faced, then maybe I would too.

As Maya Angelou finished reading her last poem, I looked back out into the audience. I stood up and leaned over the railing in front of me and looked down. Every single eye in the room was on her. Papi tugged at my shirt.

"Sit down. Pay attention," he said.

"I am. This is incredible. All of these people are here for *her*."

"I know. Now shh."

I sat and listened to Maya's final lines: "Now you understand / Just why my head's not bowed. / . . . 'Cause I'm a woman / Phenomenally. / Phenomenal woman. / That's me." She nodded her head briefly, closed her book and said thank you. The entire room stood up and burst into applause. I jumped up and down and cheered as if I were at a basketball game. I had never felt so exhilarated in my life. Papi put his hand on my shoulder, and I looked up at him. He was nodding his head and smiling.

In that moment, I knew there was more to my life than what I had been through or what I was living. I was more than just a black Dominican girl who struggled to fit in. I was more than my body hair or my unibrow or what my family wanted me to be. I could be anyone or anything I really wanted to be. And I was determined to make a difference because I wanted to make Mami and Papi proud. I wanted Papi to one day see me and smile the way he was smiling now.

I saw how Maya Angelou's story affected people and I knew the many ways she had changed me. I decided then that if Maya Angelou could be the author of her own story and rewrite her destiny to become a phenomenal woman, then somehow, in some way, so could I.

ALSO BY JASMINNE MENDEZ

City without Altar

Josefina's Habichuelas / Las habichuelas de Josefina

Island of Dreams

Night-Blooming Jasmin(n)e